CLE/N Theatr
BRE/\K Clwyd

THICK AS THIEVES

by Katherine Chandler

Thick As Thieves was first performed at
Theatr Clwyd on 11 October 2018.

THICK AS THIEVES
by Katherine Chandler

CAST

GAIL   Polly Frame
KAREN   Siwan Morris

CREATIVE TEAM

Director	Róisín McBrinn
Designer	Alyson Cummins
Lighting Designer	Azusa Ono
Sound Designer	Elena Peña
Producer (Clean Break)	Alison Hargreaves
Producer (Theatr Clwyd)	William James
Company Stage Manager	Jade Gooch
Deputy Stage Manager	Emily Hewlett
Production Photographers	Bronwen Sharp
	& Selina Mayer

The *Thick As Thieves* team would like to thank:

All of the staff and volunteers at both Clean Break and Theatr Clwyd, Bronwen Sharp, Selina Mayer, Diveen Henry, Isaura Barbé-Brown, Mared Swain, Caron Laban Jeeves, Isabelle Laban Jeeves, Scarlett Laban Jeeves, Olivia Laban Jeeves and all of the women at HMP Holloway who so generously shared their time and their stories with us.

Foreword
Róisín McBrinn, Tamara Harvey

It's funny where chance can lead you. It was an autumnal day, after a celebration of the wonderful theatre life of Lawrence Harbottle, that two directors bumped into each other on a busy Tube. Tamara was beginning her journey as Artistic Director of Clwyd and Róisín had just got her feet under the desk at Clean Break as their new Head of Artistic Programme. Full of the energy of having celebrated a life dedicated to theatre and playwrights, and our new posts, we started talking about the future.

Along her crash course into criminal justice, Róisín had been shocked to find out that there is no prison for women in Wales – Tamara took up post at Clwyd just as it was confirmed that the new 'super prison' in Wrexham would not take women prisoners. The average distance of a woman in prison in the UK from her home is a huge 66 miles but Welsh women are frequently even further away from their families: in 2007, the Welsh Affairs Committee reported that the average distance from home for Welsh adult women was 101 miles. Women in south Wales are taken to HMP Eastwood Park in Gloucestershire (almost four hours from Swansea by public transport) while women in north Wales go to HMP Styal in Cheshire (around three hours from Mold by public transport). These figures do not, of course, reflect the negative cultural and possible linguistic impacts that this geographic division can cause on women's lives.

Together we felt compelled to find a way to combine our companies' energies, and dedication to new plays, to commission a Welsh play about the lives of women affected by the criminal justice system. Katherine Chandler, Wales's leading female playwright and a long-term collaborator of Róisín's, was the perfect fit.

Cast

POLLY FRAME | GAIL

Polly Frame trained at Bristol University.

Theatre credits includes: *On the Exhale* (Traverse; Fringe First winner); *Jekyll & Hyde* (English Touring Consortium); *A Short History of Tractors in Ukranian* (Hull Truck); *Frankenstein, Hedda Gabler* (Northern Stage); *Henry V* (Regent's Park Open Air Theatre), *The Odyssey* (English Touring Theatre); *Mermaid* (Shared Experience); *Arcadia* (Tobacco Factory); *Twelfth Night, A Response to Twelfth Night* (Filter); *Pastoral* (Soho); *After Miss Julie* (Young Vic); *The Crossing, 66 Books* (Bush); *The Comedy of Errors* (Stafford Shakespeare Festival); *Earthquakes in London* (RNT); *The Count of Monte Cristo* (West Yorkshire Playhouse); *Macbeth* (Chichester/West End/Broadway); *Home-Work* (Bodies in Flight for Singapore Esplanade); *The Prime of Miss Jean Brodie, Poor Mrs Pepys* (New Vic); *ACDC* (Royal Court); *Cleansed* (Arcola).

Television credits include: *Doctors, Casualty, Man Down, The Tunnel, Coronation Street, Holby City, The Curse of the Hope Diamond, Silent Witness, EastEnders, Bunny Town, Sea of Souls, Accused, Life Begins, New Tricks, Meet the Magoons, The Giblets, Servants*.

Film credits include: *Macbeth, Half Light, Duplicity*.

SIWAN MORRIS | KAREN

Theatre includes: *Highway One* (Wales Millennium Centre); *Dublin Carol, Cloakroom* (Sherman Cymru); *Bird* (Royal Exchange/Sherman Cymru); *Violence and Son, Gas Station Angel* (Royal Court); *Tonypandemonium, A Good Night Out in the Valleys* (National Theatre Wales); *Knives in Hens* (Theatre Royal, Bath); *A Midsummer Night's Dream, Suddenly Last Summer, The Rabbit, King Lear, Flora's War, Hosts of Rebecca, The Journey of Mary Kelly, Rape of the Fair Country, Equus* (Theatr Clwyd); *The Seagull* (Bristol Old Vic); *Much Ado About Nothing, Twelfth Night* (UK tour); *The Merchant of Venice, The Winter's Tale* (Ludlow Festival).

Television includes: *Gwaith/Cartref, Y Streica Fi, Doctor Who, Our Girl, Wolfblood, Holby City, Whites, Caerdydd, Con Passionate, Miss Marple, Skins, Antigone, Mine All Mine, 20 Things To Do Before You're 30, Belonging, Social Action, The Bill, Casualty, Mind To Kill, The Bench, Tales of the Pleasure Beach*.

Film includes: *Dark Signal, The Devil's Vice, The Machine, Sister Lulu, sucker fish, The Marvellous Handshake*.

Radio includes: *Summer is Long to Come, Dylan Thomas Shorts, Dover & the Unkindest Cut of All, On Top of the World, Same As it Ever Was, Station Road, The True Memoirs of Harriett Wilson*.

Creative Team

KATHERINE CHANDLER | WRITER

Katherine Chandler is an award-winning writer working in theatre, film and television.

Twice a finalist for the prestigious Susan Smith Blackburn prize with her plays *Before it Rains* and *Parallel Lines*, Katherine is also a recipient of the Theatre Critics of Wales, Writers' Guild Playwright Award and Creative Wales Award.

Katherine was awarded the Judges Prize in the Bruntwood Prize for Playwriting for her play *Bird*.

Bird was co-produced by Manchester Royal Exchange and Sherman Theatre, a first collaboration between the two companies, and received critical acclaim at a national level.

Katherine was the inaugural winner of the BBC and National Theatre Wales, Wales Drama Award and has worked a number of times with both companies. Her adaptation of Terry Jones' fairy tales *The Silly Kings* for National Theatre Wales won the Best Show for Young People at the 2014 Theatre Critics of Wales Awards and her NHS70 play *Peggy's Song* is currently in production with the company.

BBC iPlayer released Katherine's first film, *Tag*, as part of the BBC3/BBC iPlayer drama launch. She has attended BBC Drama shadow schemes for both *EastEnders* and *Casualty*.

Katherine's most recent works have been produced by companies such as Clean Break Theatre Company, National Theatre Wales, National Theatre Connections, Theatr Clwyd, Sherman Theatre, Bristol Old Vic and Manchester Royal Exchange Theatre.

Currently Katherine is working on a variety of exciting commissions with companies such as National Theatre Wales, Sherman Theatre, Clean Break, Nottingham Playhouse, Theatr Clwyd and the BBC.

RÓISÍN MCBRINN | DIRECTOR

Róisín McBrinn is the Joint Artistic Director of Clean Break, and a theatre director with over fifteen years experience working in the UK, Ireland and internationally. During her time with Clean Break she has directed *Joanne* (Soho/RSC); *House/Amongst The Reeds* (The Yard) and *Thick As Thieves* (Theatr Clwyd) for the company. She was formerly Associate Director at Sherman Cymru where she oversaw the commissioning and developing of new Welsh writing. Róisín has directed for the Donmar Warehouse (*Noveccento*), Sheffield Theatres (*Afterplay*), West Yorkshire Playhouse (*Yerma*), Prime Cut (*Villa/Discurso*), The Abbey Theatre (*No Escape*, *Perve*, *Heartbreak House*). She has developed new work for Soho Theatre, the National Theatre, the Bush, The Abbey and Sherman Theatre. This summer she directed a stage adaptation of Roddy Doyle's *The Snapper* for Dublin's Gate Theatre.

ALYSON CUMMINS | DESIGNER

Designs include *The Lion in Winter* (English Theatre Frankfurt); *Così Fan Tutte*, *Zazà* (Opera Holland Park); *Tosca* (Icelandic Opera); *Eyes Closed Ears Covered* (Bunker); *Jacques Brel is Alive and Well* (Gate, Dublin); *Sinners, The Nativity* & *The Gingerbread Mix-Up, Pentecost, Mixed Marriage* (Lyric Belfast); *The Nest* (Lyric Belfast/Young Vic); *Fabric* (Robin Rayner/Marlowe); *Macbeth* (Iford*); This Limetree Bower* (Project); *The Lighthouse* (Linbury Studio); *The Night Alive* (DTF/Lyric Belfast); *Heartbreak House, The Risen People, Quietly, Perve, No Escape* (Abbey Theatre); *Be Infants in Evil* (Druid); *Summertime* (Tinderbox); *It's a Family Affair* (Sherman Cymru); *Before It Rains* (Bristol Old Vic/Sherman Cymru) and *Pornography* (Waking Exploits).

AZUSA ONO | LIGHTING DESIGNER

Azusa Ono has been creating lighting design for a range of live performances and art forms, challenging the boundary of the theatre frame by widening and shifting the perspective through lighting. She trained in fine arts in Japan and lighting design at the Royal Central School of Speech and Drama in London in 2003–07.

Recent credits include: *Effigies of Wickedness* (Gate/ENO); *Smack That* (The Pit, Barbican/national tour); *Tate Live Exhibition – Joan Jonas* (Tate Modern); *Yvette* (Royal Festival Hall/national tour); *Cuttin' It* (Young Vic/national tour); *Kairos Opera* (V&A); *Becoming Invisible* (Bascule Chamber Tower Bridge); *Killer* (Shoreditch Town Hall); *Darkness Darkness* (Nottingham Playhouse); *I Know All The Secrets In My World* (Derby Theatre/ tour); *Dot, Squiggle and Rest* (Royal Opera House Clore Studio); *Peddling* (New York 59E59/national tour); *We Are Proud...* (Bush); *The Love Song of Alfred J Hitchcock* (Curve Leicester/international tour);*Copyright Christmas* (Barbican Centre) and *Fanfared* (Crucible Sheffield).

www.ald.org.uk/azusaonoa

ELENA PEÑA | SOUND DESIGNER

Theatrical design credits include: *Misty* (Bush); *All of Me* (China Plate); *How I Hacked My Way Into Space* (Unlimited Theatre/tour); *The Suicide* (Arts Ed); *The Caretaker* (Bristol Old Vic/Northampton Royal & Derngate); *Thebes Land* (Arcola); *Pixel Dust* and *Wonder* (Edinburgh Festival); *HIR* (Bush); *The Vacuum Cleaner Project* (One Tenth Human & Hear Me Roar, Nuffield Lancaster); *Boat* (Company Three, Battersea Arts Centre); *Years of Sunlight* (Theatre503); *The Bear/The Proposal* (Young Vic); *Layla's Room, The Muddy Choir, What The Thunder Said, The Littlest Quirky* (Theatre Centre); *Sleepless* (Shoreditch Town Hall, Analogue Theatre, Staatstheatre Mainz).

Sound Installation: *Have Your Circumstances Changed?, Yes These Eyes Are The Windows* (Art Angel)

Elena is an Associate Artist for Inspector Sands where her credits include: *The Lounge* (Summer Hall, Edinburgh – Offie nomination for Best Sound Design); *Rock Pool* and *Seochon Odyssey* (HiSeoul Fetsival, Korea); *A High Street Odyssey* (UK tour).

CLEAN BREAK

WHO WE ARE

Clean Break is a theatre company committed to shining a light on the injustices women experience both in and beyond the criminal justice system. Working with the finest female playwrights and theatrical artists in the UK, we create bold, insightful theatre that urges debate, deepens understanding and connects audiences with women's stories, often for the first time.

'As an artist my commission with Clean Break has inspired and sustained me creatively in brilliant and unexpected ways.'
Lucy Kirkwood, Olivier Award Winner and Patron

WHAT WE DO

Alongside our professional productions, our creative learning programme offers unparalleled opportunities to women in prisons and the community. We provide members with a foundation of learning and skills in theatre performance, creativity and wellbeing, as well as chances to engage in professional, public- facing performances. By connecting women with exceptional artists we help them to find their voices, aim high and pursue their ambitions.

'It was a breath of fresh air; it took me out of here and helped me to imagine something better.' *Participant at HMP Low Newton*

SUPPORT US

If you'd like to help us use theatre to change lives, please visit our website, **www.cleanbreak.org.uk**

'I've seen the impact of Clean Break's work... it is an organisation that changes lives and changes minds.' *Dame Harriet Walter DBE, Patron*

KEEP IN TOUCH

Be first in the know for all Clean Break's news by signing up to our newsletter via our website, or follow us on our social media channels:

Twitter: @CleanBrk
Facebook: /cleanbreak
Instagram: @CleanBrk

Clean Break Staff List

Producer	Alison Hargreaves
Joint Artistic Director	Anna Herrmann
Digital Coordinator	Ashleigh-Rose Harman
Support Manager	Carole Jarvis
Marketing Coordinator	Caroline Boss
Development and Members Assistant	Demi Wilson-Smith
Administrator	Dezh Zhelyazkova
Development Manager	Emily Goodyer
Executive Director	Erin Gavaghan
Head of Participation	Jacqueline Stewart
Receptionist	Katherine Sturt-Scobie
Head of Operations	Khaz Khan
Head of Finance & Business	Laura Mallows
Senior Development Manager	Lillian Ashford
Participation Manager	Lorraine Maher
Executive Assistant	Maya Ellis
Studio Administrator	Rachel Tookey
Joint Artistic Director	Róisín McBrinn
Head of Development & Communications	Sally Muckley
Volunteer Co-ordinator	Samantha McNeil
Finance & Data Manager	Selina Mayer

Clean Break
2 Patshull Road
London
NW5 2LB
Registered company number 2690758
Registered charity number 1017560

Tel: 020 7482 8600
Fax: 020 7482 8611
general@cleanbreak.org.uk
www.cleanbreak.org.uk

Theatr Clwyd

ABOUT THEATR CLWYD

'One of the hidden treasures of North Wales, a huge vibrant culture complex' *Guardian*

Theatr Clwyd is one of the foremost producing theatres in Wales – a beacon of excellence looking across the Clwydian Hills yet only forty minutes from Liverpool.

Since 1976 it has been a theatrical powerhouse and much-loved home for the community. Now, led by the Executive team of Tamara Harvey and Liam Evans-Ford, it is going from strength to strength producing world-class theatre, from new plays to classic revivals.

There are three theatre spaces, a cinema, café, bar and art galleries and, alongside its own shows, it offers a rich and varied programme of visual arts, film, theatre, music, dance and comedy. Theatr Clwyd works extensively with the local community, schools and colleges and creates award-winning work for, with and by young people. In the past two years it has co-produced with the Sherman Theatre, Hijinx, Gagglebabble and The Other Room in Cardiff, Paines Plough, Vicky Graham Productions, HighTide, Hampstead Theatre, Bristol Old Vic, The Rose Theatre, Kingston, Headlong, Sheffield Theatres, the Orange Tree Theatre, English Touring Theatre and National Theatre, amongst others.

In 2016/17 over 420,000 people saw a Theatr Clwyd production, in the building and across the UK.

Theatr Clwyd yw un o theatrau cynhyrchu mwyaf blaenllaw Cymru – yn batrwm o ragoriaeth yn edrych draw dros Fryniau Clwyd ond eto ddim ond deugain munud o Lerpwl.

Ers 1976 rydym wedi bod yn bwerdy theatrig ac yn gartref poblogaidd iawn i'n cymuned. Nawr, o dan arweiniad y tîm Gweithredol newydd, Tamara Harvey a Liam Evans-Ford, rydym yn mynd o nerth i nerth gan gynhyrchu theatr o safon byd, o ddramâu newydd i adfywio'r clasuron.

Mae gennym dair theatr, sinema, caffi, bar ac orielau celf ac, ochr yn ochr â'n sioeau ein hunain, rydym yn cynnig rhaglen gyfoethog ac amrywiol o gelfyddydau gweledol, ffilm, theatr, cerddoriaeth, dawns a chomedi. Rydym yn gweithio'n helaeth gyda'n cymuned leol, ysgolion a cholegau ac yn creu gwaith llwyddiannus iawn ar gyfer, gyda a gan bobl ifanc. Yn ystod y ddwy flynedd diwethaf rydym wedi cynhyrchu ar y cyd gyda Theatr y Sherman, Hijinx, Gagglebabble a The Other Room yng Nghaerdydd, Paines Plough, Vicky Graham Productions, HighTide, Hampstead Theatre, Bristol Old Vic, The Rose Theatre, Kingston, Headlong, Sheffield Theatres, Orange Tree Theatre, yr English Touring Theatre, y National Theatre, ynghyd âg eraill.

Yn ystod 2016/17 daeth dros 420,000 o bobl i weld un o gynyrchiadau Theatr Clwyd, yn yr adeilad a thros y DU.

Interview with Katherine Chandler

What was it like to write for Clean Break; how is it different from being commissioned by other companies?

I have loved working with the company for lots of reasons. It is a different experience from working with any other company because of the process. I spent a lot of time initially at Clean Break with the women who were attending classes there, and then spent time at Holloway Prison with a different group of women who were there.

I tried to go in to my time at both places without any thoughts about what I wanted to write about, and really just came out with a lot of ideas.

There was always, in both groups, continuous reference to kids and family, and although we didn't talk directly about anyone's stories – because we were there for workshops about theatre – kids were a big thing and were always being mentioned in chat.

It made me think a lot about motherhood and separation and the immediate judgements we make about each other based on generalised, ingrained ways of thinking, and just the way we judge each other about our mothering whoever, whatever we are, so I was interested to challenge that a bit.

The commission was for two companies, Clean Break and Theatr Clwyd, so that was also a consideration when I was thinking about the play because the two companies have different identities so the play had to fit with both. I just felt that I wanted to write a really big, small play!

I would say that when I had the seeds of an idea I wrote a first draft very quickly, and then have spent a long time redrafting. Normally my plays are between three and six drafts and this play is currently on draft ten. It's a play with a cast of two so I felt the script had to be really tight, it's like a game of tennis with dialogue – every word counts – so it's taken time to get it right.

I also seem to start a play with a first draft that has murders and overly dramatic things happening and then through the drafting process the true story emerges, which in this case was a reconnection of two sisters that were estranged.

What are you hoping audiences will go home thinking about after seeing Thick As Thieves*?*

I hope they go away having been entertained for an hour or so. Then if they think a bit about mothers and how we regard each other, that would be good. Themes that run through are also about our starting points in life, paths we take, helping each other, judgement, class and family. I hope it might provoke thoughts about any of those things but I'm happy if they just like it!

What have you taken away from your experience of writing Thick As Thieves, *and will it impact any of your future work?*

I feel very satisfied with the play now and when I hear it I can see the influences of my time with Clean Break and the women. It was an experience that I really value and I won't forget it or the women. I think it's been a really interesting way of working. For me, all my plays are different and I think the process of your current one is likely to impact the way you write the next one, in one way or another. The play I wrote after *Thick As Thieves* was a completely fictional, comedic monologue that I went in to with a solid structure and was written in two drafts, it couldn't have been more different! I enjoy the differences. The next project I'm working on is similar in the process to *Thick As Thieves.*

THICK AS THIEVES

Katherine Chandler

Acknowledgements

Thanks to Róisín McBrinn and Tamara Harvey.

And Siwan Morris and Polly Frame.

K.C.

To Guy, Mali and Mathonwy
Always for you

4

Characters

GAIL
KAREN

This text went to press before the end of rehearsals and so may differ slightly from the play as performed.

One

The Factory

Although the scene is real and a single incident, it's also surreal and a representation of many incidents in GAIL*'s life. The many times that she has come up against broken rules and routines and closing doors and second chances.*

It should reflect the chaos she has in her thoughts and the cycle of obstacles she faces repeatedly.

*A radio can play. On and off. Nina Simone songs come in and out. A variety but must have 'My Baby Just Cares for Me' within the mix. White noise and levels of louder volume as and when useful to suggest absurdity. A buzz might be helpful.
A door might slam off somewhere. The lights flicker/dim. A door might lock.*

There might be a chair or a desk that would suggest an office/something official.

Between her dialogue, which is directed at random members of the audience, GAIL *will do all or some of the following:*

Wait.

Fidget.

Sit up and down, out and in, of the chair.

Pick at herself.

Drum her fingers.

Jump.

Turn around.

Get confused.

Rub her eyes.

Turn and stand with her back to the audience.

Sniff.

Fuss her hair.

Circle the space.

Sniff again.

Clear her throat.

Be bothered by her nose.

Hum. 'My baby...'

Childish formula dancing.

Wipe her nose with the back of her hand.

Look at the back of her hand. Shit, shouldn't have done that.

Wipe her hand in her skirt.

Look around.

Rub down her clothes.

GAIL *is onstage. Alone. Waiting. She paces. Circles. In her own time she finds her place. Directs her dialogue at audience members. Using all of the audience. Moving at the reset.*

GAIL   I know you said to phone.

            But. You know.

            By the time I call.

            Sorry. I am. I'm sorry.

            How late was I?

            Five minutes?

            Twenty-five.

            Okay, well I thought it was less so.

            Sounds break into the scene. The radio changes.
            The lights are brighter/dimmer.

GAIL *resets*.

I was going to call, it's just…

I didn't so.

Okay, well.

I know that, I just thought.

I thought it was less.
I thought.
About ten or something
like that.

Last time?

I don't remember that.

There's nothing wrong with my memory.

Alright?

Sounds break in.

GAIL *resets*.

I think it is, yeah.

Sorry. I am. I'm sorry.

But. You know.

People like me?

I know. And I'm grateful, miss.

I need this.

Yeah. Yes.

It does.

It does help.

And I'm grateful.

Sounds break in.

GAIL *resets*.

It won't happen again. I swear.

Four minutes? Was I?

That was a piss. I'll bet that was it.

I mean, come on.

I was an hour late on the 23rd.

If you wanna do me for late.
Make it a good one at least.

I do try.

I did.

Sounds break in.

GAIL *resets*.

It's not excuses.

It's not. I'm just telling you.

It's reasons.

Things happen. To me they do.

I'm not lying.

I know.

I was offered the position in good faith. I was.

Decency?

I'm decent.

Come on.
Miss.
Please.

Sounds break in.

GAIL *resets*.

I know all about honesty.

You saying I'm not honest?

I value it too.

You haven't got the what's-it-called on that.
Honesty.

Poor attendance? Yeah well.

Performance?

I can read.

I said, I'm sorry.

Look. I'm sorry alright.

Don't.

Sounds break in.

GAIL *resets.*

I know all about the disciplinary action.

I didn't attend that meeting, so.

It's not what you're thinking.

I tried.

I got the letter, I said…

And that, the attatchment, I got that.

And I was gonna phone to discuss the stuff what it
said.

I was.

I know that now.

I don't know why.

*Sounds break in. 'My Baby Just Cares for Me' is in
among them.*

GAIL *resets.*

Four weeks' notice?

What now? From now?

What about the four weeks?

And that's it?

Payment in what?

Where will you forward it?

I don't know, do I.

I worked hard.

I did.

Sometimes things… it's not excuses. I'm just saying, you got it wrong.

You got me wrong.

It's not right this.

Thirty days to appeal?

Does that work, does it?

You reckon that's gonna work?

Okay, I see it. I can read, you know.

Yeah, well.

Well…

Here we go again.

Sounds break in.

The lights flicker/change/radio changes to loud white noise

A loud buzz.

GAIL *starts to hum over the buzz: 'My Baby Just Cares for Me'.*

Half-hearted foot moves. Hand taps. Taking us into…

Two

The Office

GAIL *lightly whistles 'My Baby Just Cares for Me'.*

End of day.

Early evening.

Deserted office.

KAREN *is at her desk.*

GAIL *taps at door.*

GAIL   I was out there for a while so I

KAREN   Right. Yes.

GAIL   Nobody said nothing to me. I just came in.

KAREN   Oh. Right.

GAIL   You might wanna think about your security there, Kaz, you know in today's climate, with terrorists and that.

KAREN   I don't think there's any need for that.

GAIL   Yeah.
Perhaps they thought I worked here.
A cleaner or something.

KAREN   Gail.
Sorry, I was…

GAIL   You're a busy lady.

KAREN   Yes.
Come in
I'm.
God.
Look, sorry
It's been a long day…

GAIL   Look at you.

KAREN   Ceri said…

GAIL   You look good, Kaz.

KAREN   She said – Do I? Thank you – Ceri said –

          Pauses.

          She said there was someone –

          Pauses.

          Takes a breath.

          It's out of the blue
          you know…

GAIL   Yeah.

KAREN   It's a surprise…

GAIL   Nice office.

KAREN   I mean… thanks… but You.
          Coming here

GAIL   You got your name on the door and everything.

KAREN   Don't get me wrong.
          It's – the name-on-the-door thing's a bit… but
          It is a bit
          It's unexpected isn't it? This?

GAIL   You changed your name.

          Pause.

KAREN   Yes.
          Well.
          You know, just
          Everyone calls me Kate.
          So.

GAIL   Not Karen, any more.

KAREN   No.
          No.
          Not really
          Not any more

          Pause.

          Not for a long time really.

GAIL   Made it hard to find you, did that.

KAREN   Really?
            You found me though.

GAIL   Yeah.

            I keep in touch with Teresa.
            She's got grandkids, you know. She had her first
            one when she was thirty-four, said she pretty much
            brings 'em up by all accounts, don't mind though,
            they're good kids.
            And Dorian.
            Remember him?
            He was inside last I heard and his sisters too.
            They was around for a while but I haven't seen
            none of them in donkey's years, so.
            I don't know where the others ended up.
            It was Teresa told me about you.
            Told me she run into you in town a couple of
            months ago.
            With your husband.
            Said he was a lawyer or something.
            Kids.
            Said you'd just moved back here with your fancy
            job. She said she wasn't sure it was you at first cos
            your husband was calling you Kate.
            But it was you alright.

            When she told me what your new name was and
            that you was working for the council, well, it was
            easy enough then.

            I googled you.

            Googled me and all.

            There's a few of me around, Kaz.
            Should see them. Professors and all sorts.

            One of them was a porn director. That's about right
            that. (*Laughs.*) That's what I thought.

            Gail Palmer. Interior designers and everything.

I wasn't there though. Not the actual me.

(*Laughs*.) That could be a blessing though. What's
someone gonna write about me, aye.
Dread to think.

You came up straight away though, with all quotes
and policies and strategies and all that. Dead
important you was. That's what I thought when
I seen it. There was an actress as well. A comedian.
I didn't know her.

But you though.

There was a big photo of you saying you was the
new Head of Children's Services.

KAREN   I said I didn't want a photo.
It's all a bit – I don't know why they needed – it's
embarrassing really.
PR and
I never like doing the photo things but on that one
– I don't know if it's appropriate – you know, I'll
have to tell them –

Takes a breath.

It was for a charity campaign so
Look…
Gail,

Pause.

Takes a breath.

This – it's knocked me sideways a bit.
I have to say.

GAIL   It's been a long time.

KAREN   Yes.

Stops.

Is there a reason you're here, Gail?

GAIL   It's a nice room, you got.

KAREN   It's just if you wanted to speak with me

GAIL   Speak with you?
        I did want to 'speak with you'

KAREN   You could have arranged a time.
        I just
        You know
        Coming out of the blue like this.

        Pause.

GAIL   Oh sorry, Kaz. Course.
        I didn't realise.

KAREN   It's fine.
        It's just I'm so busy.

GAIL   Yeah. God. What am I like, just turning up?

KAREN   It's not.
        It's fine really.

GAIL   I should have made an appointment?

KAREN   Well, appointment sounds...

GAIL   Yeah. I did try to contact you a bit.

KAREN   Oh.

GAIL   After I saw Teresa, you know.
        But I couldn't get hold of you.
        Even tried to get on your Facebook an' all.

KAREN   You can arrange to see me with Ceri on the desk.

GAIL   Yeah, I did try to do that.
        Your diary is chocka there, Kaz, that's what she said.
        I thought though,
        I'd just come and see you.
        You know.

KAREN   Yes.
        Well
        Today's been crazy.
        Hectic.

GAIL   Yeah, I seen that.

KAREN   I had a
        It's madness really
        You know
        This week's been really tough.

GAIL   So I just waited on that chair there outside. I been
        there most of the day.

KAREN   There's important things that – Actually this
        month's been, this year even –

GAIL   And then everyone was leaving. And that Ceri, she
        told me I had to leave with everyone.

KAREN   It's a busy job.

GAIL   So I walked out with them all.

KAREN   You can imagine.

GAIL   But then I come back in. I thought I'd check that
        you was still here.

KAREN   I am.

GAIL   I can see that.

KAREN   I'm usually here until the others
        Ceri goes
        Generally Ceri goes and then
        After that I leave.

GAIL   Children's Services though? It's funny that, don't
        you think? You, ending up working in the care
        system.

KAREN   Is it?
        I never thought about it really.

        Thinks.

        Maybe.

GAIL   Made me laugh a bit. But then I s'pose. Maybe it's
        a good thing.

KAREN   Right.
          Is Ceri there, at all?

GAIL   She went a while back.

KAREN   I didn't see her go?

GAIL   You didn't notice?

KAREN   Is there anyone in the office?

GAIL   They've all gone home.
          Just you and me.

KAREN   And Bill? Bill will be around.

GAIL   It is late to be working this is, Kaz.

KAREN   I work long hours.

GAIL   That Ceri.
          Is she your right-hand man is she?

KAREN   Ceri's my PA.

          She's very good, as it goes.

GAIL   Is she? I dunno.

KAREN   What?

GAIL   Look, it's not for me to say.

          But if I'm honest with you, Karen, your girl there's
          a bit jobsworthy I reckon.

KAREN   Ceri?

GAIL   Cos I phoned Monday and she said she'd get back
          to me, I said, I told her who it was. I told her to
          tell you.
          She didn't get back to me though, which I don't
          think is that good actually.

KAREN   That's really not like Ceri.

GAIL   I tried again then on Tuesday. A few times, mind you.

          And all day Wednesday an' all.

KAREN   She's the best PA I've had.

GAIL   She wouldn't put me through is what I think
         happened.

KAREN   I'm sure that's not what happened.

GAIL   Did she tell you?

         Pause.

KAREN   She knows not to
         If I'm on a difficult case
         Anyone.
         She won't put anyone through.

GAIL   Are you on a difficult case?

KAREN   Yes.

GAIL   Well.
         Okay then
         but she could have got back to me though.

KAREN   She probably
         She forgot, is all it is.

GAIL   A bit rude though, Karen.
         That's what I think.

         Pause.

KAREN   Look, Gail, I hope you don't mind but I've been in
         meetings all day and actually my head is thumping.

GAIL   Yeah, she said about your meetings.

KAREN   I did say for you to come back another day.

         *Starts looking through her drawers and bag for
         paracetamol.*

GAIL   She told me to come back tomorrow.

KAREN   Well, there we go.

GAIL   But then when she went to the loo, I thought I'd
         check your appointment book, save wasting my

time and coming back all this way. Good job I did
cos it looked like you was out of the building all
day tomorrow.

Well then I thought, you got the weekend, so we'd
be into next week.

KAREN   I don't know about that.
I'm just
I just operate on a day-by-day basis at the moment.

Finds paracetamol.

Oh, thank God.

Takes water bottle out of her bag.

GAIL   Oh.
I see.
Everything okay though?

KAREN   Everything's fine, thank you.

Opens bottle of water.

GAIL   Monday you got a hospital appointment. So we're
into next Tuesday or whatever.

Pause.

You okay, are you?

KAREN *takes tablets.*

KAREN   I'm fine.

Look this isn't great for me
I need to get off so
It's really great and everything that you looked me
up but
As you can see this isn't such a good time.

GAIL   I live just round the corner from there. The
hospital.

Pause.

KAREN   That's a long way from here.

GAIL   I like walking. I walk for miles. Sometimes I'll
              walk around all day. That's why I'm so thin.
              Look at me.
              Like a gypsy's dog, all bone and skin.

              We used to walk for miles, didn't we.
              When we was kids.
              We'd do anything to get out and about, me and you.
              Away from that place they put us.
              Remember?
              It was freedom, weren't it.

              What you at the hospital for?

KAREN   Really, you shouldn't be looking at private things.

GAIL   Nothing serious, is it?

KAREN   Nothing for you to
              It's not important.

GAIL   It's in your book.

KAREN   I was thinking of cancelling.
              I'm so
              I'm extremely busy.

GAIL   You shouldn't make work more important than
              whatever it is you was going to the hospital for,
              Karen.

              You always was fickle.

KAREN   I wasn't. I'm not.

GAIL   Couldn't make up your mind.

KAREN   I'm very decisive, actually.

GAIL   You've changed, a lot, I know that for nothing.

KAREN   Well, I'm not thirteen now.

GAIL   No.

KAREN   I'm a different person. Thank God.

GAIL   I would have known you anywhere.

KAREN   Really? I don't know that I'd have recognised you.

Pause.

GAIL   You done good though, haven't you.

KAREN   I've worked hard.

GAIL   You been lucky, Kaz.

KAREN   Is there a reason you want to see me, Gail?

GAIL   Sorry, not Kaz.
Kate.
It's gonna take some getting used to that, I can tell you…

Pause.

It's different, Kate.

KAREN   You say that like it's something I should be ashamed of.

GAIL   Goes with you though
Matches with your life.
Now.
This life.

I knew. I always knew you'd make something of yourself.
I did think you would.
I hoped you did anyways.
I hoped you was alright.

KAREN   I'm not ashamed of moving on.

GAIL   You shouldn't be.
I'm dead proud of you
'Kate'. I'll get used to it.

KAREN   Kate's not that different from Karen. It sort of evolved.
I'm not – Proud? –
I'm not
I don't need your pride, Gail.

My name is Kate.
I don't hide Karen.
It's just been that way for twenty-odd years. It took
me through school and uni and
look
I'm just an average woman with a career, kids,
a husband.
My life is normal.
Full of school timetables and washing and what
we're having for dinner and after-school clubs and
loading the dishwasher and weekends and.
And.
It's just turned out this way.
This is who I am.
It's not then and

Pause.

I'm just
I'm just me.

I'm not hiding.

GAIL *processes that.*

GAIL   Do they know about me?

KAREN   Who?

GAIL   Your husband? The kids?

Pause.

KAREN   Not really.

GAIL   Not really? You tell them about their auntie?

KAREN   No.

Holds a look.

KAREN *looks away.*

Pause.

GAIL   Is that your kids?
           In that photo.

KAREN   Yes.

GAIL   Three.

KAREN   Yes.

GAIL   I thought three.

KAREN   Did you?

GAIL   I sort of guessed about that.
         I did wonder if you're that kind of type now.

KAREN   That type?

GAIL   I don't know.
         You.
         You seem like.
         I don't know.

KAREN   What?

GAIL   All chia (*Pronounces it 'ch-eye-ah'*.) seeds,
         avocados, three kids.
         Like that.

KAREN   I don't eat chia (*Pronounces it 'chee-a'*.) seeds.

GAIL   Kale then, purple sprouting broccoli and all that
         stuff that they eats. Superfoods. They loves their
         superfoods.
         It's a type.

KAREN   Having three children is a type?

GAIL   Yeah. And 'scuse the language, Karen, but what the
         fuck, pray tell me, is baby yoga?

         Finds herself funny.

KAREN   Does that go along with the three kids, does it?

GAIL   It's like two isn't enough.
         They wants to show everyone how much they loves
         being a mother so they goes for three.
         And big cars.
         They loves their big cars, don't they.

KAREN   Do they?

GAIL   And on these roads.
          We're not America though, are we, Kaz?

KAREN   Perhaps they do love being a mother.
          Perhaps that's a thing.

GAIL   Maybe.
          Maybe they do.
          Ah, ignore me.
          I'm only messing with you.
          Too much time on my hands is the problem.

          It does seem like a thing though, don't it.

KAREN   It's not a thing, Jesus, Gail.

GAIL   It'll all change again soon enough, anyway. When
          the likes of me starts eating kale and chia seeds
          they won't do it no more then.
          They'll find something else.

KAREN   Will they. Right, well that's sorted out the middle
          classes then.
          Look
          Gail, I'm sorry but
          I really do need to go home.

GAIL   Bet those three girls of yours don't have to share
          like we did.

          KAREN *gathers her things together.*

KAREN   The little ones share. They're very close.

GAIL   Remember though.
          Me and you in that room.

KAREN   Not really.

          GAIL *starts doing a funny version of 'My Baby
          Just Cares for Me'.*

GAIL   'Ba doom da boom da boom, boom, boom,
          boom...' Remember, Kaz?

Does a silly dance as she sings – tries to engage an awkward KAREN.

She sings the first couple of lines of the song.

We used to do that dance? That one. With the feet thing. And you used to nod your head like you was…
I dunno, like…

Shows KAREN.

My baby just cares for me

Like this, remember?

Exaggerates the dance – tries to get KAREN *in it.*

Sings the next two lines of the song.

We loved that song. We'd sing it to each other? You remember?

KAREN   No, I'm not sure I do.

KAREN*'s really not into the song or* GAIL, *very uncomfortable for her.*

GAIL *stops.*

Shrugs.

GAIL   We was always. Playing it. Singing it.

GAIL *picks up photo.*

Your kids are pretty.

GAIL *smiles at the photo, maybe touches the glass.*

KAREN *stops.*

Watches GAIL.

They're beautiful, Kaz.
They look fresh.

That their school uniform?

KAREN   Um.
         I don't know. Probably.

GAIL   Not like us. We looked like scraps, didn't we?
         Right scruffy scraps we was.
         I never had any new clothes, remember.
         Always had your hand-me-downs.
         And they come from God-knows-where before you
         had 'em.

         That coat I had. That parka. With the fur and all
         that quilting in the inside. I thought I was Liam
         Gallagher.
         And the hood zipped right up over my face.
         Looked like an alien or something. Like an
         old-fashioned diver.
         I never took the hood down. Even in the summer.
         I thought I was going to pass out half the time but
         I still wouldn't take it off.

         I loved that coat.

         Back to the photo.

         They are cute though, your girls. With the pigtails
         and that.

         I'd like to meet them.

KAREN   Would you.

         KAREN *takes the photo back.*

GAIL   I would, yeah.

         I got time on my hands.

         I could meet them.

         KAREN *puts the photo in her drawer.*

         Are they like you?

KAREN   They're very bright, thriving at school. They're
         good kids. Amazing actually.

GAIL   They look like you a bit I think.

KAREN   They look like my husband.

GAIL   I could come round yours?

            No response.

            The little one there.
            She looks like she's got a bit of cheek to her, if you
            ask me.
            Like her mother, I bet.
            What's her name?

KAREN   She's like her father. She's a joy. Very sweet.

GAIL   They say that about girls, don't they? That it's
            some sort of nature thing that they look like
            their dads.

            Pause.

            The little ones are special though, ain't they. The
            baby.

            I just had two.
            Boys.
            The oldest was a mistake. He's a little sod.
            The little one was a mistake an' all but.
            I wanted him anyways.
            I really wanted him.
            I grew into the oldest. Too much like me, that's
            his problem.
            The two of them though.
            Thick as thieves they are.

            They're my world though.

KAREN   They're all special. It's an absolute privilege…
            well…

GAIL   Yeah. There's nothing quite like it is there. Being
            a mother.

            Pause.

KAREN   Why are you here, Gail?

Pause.

GAIL   After you went.
I looked for you.
Couldn't find you.

It was like you just disappeared.

I didn't stop, though. Looking for you.
They tried to stop me but.
You know me, when I get something in my head.

KAREN   I didn't know.

GAIL   And I know, you know, I know we was kids when
it all happened.
They didn't want us kicking up a fuss. I know
that now.
They made it impossible for me to find you.
But

You just went.
Like that.
And I thought.

It wasn't your fault. I know it wasn't your fault but.

There was no trace of you

KAREN   I don't want to talk about it, Gail.

GAIL   I thought you could have let me know where
you was.

Pause.

Just a note I thought.
Anything really.

KAREN   Look, I don't remember much about it.
I
I don't remember
They told me they sent you away.

GAIL   They tried.

KAREN   Scotland or somewhere, I think they said.

GAIL   Everyone's so nice up there. Friendly. Clean air.
        Fucking hated it.
        Couldn't keep me there. Kept running away.

        I missed the hall. Even missed fucking Rocking
        Roberts, remember him, Kaz. He used to get off on
        belting the shit out of us. And his sidekick. Nasty
        bitch. She was. It's a joke innit. But I missed her
        an' all.

        Then they chucked me over the water to Belfast for
        a bit.
        Thought the sea would stop me.
        But I'm like that thing. That what's-it-called from
        Australia. A boomerang.
        Water couldn't stop me.
        I was back soon enough.
        I liked Belfast better than Scotland.
        Belfast was more like here.
        I worried about you.

KAREN   I was with a good family.

GAIL   I can see.
        You're talking all posh and dressed all nice.

KAREN   A proper family.

        In Wales.

GAIL   Wales.
        Fucking hell.

KAREN   I loved it there.

GAIL   I would never have looked in Wales.

KAREN   They looked after me.
        Properly.
        Gave me a life.

        Pause.

I loved the clean air.
Everyone so friendly.
Being nice.
I thought to myself. I remember thinking to myself
you would have hated it.
We were surrounded by sea.
Beaches.
I thought about how you hated the sand.
Remember.
That time they took us on that trip to the coast.
I think it was the first time we'd ever seen a beach.
Sand.
You had that coat on for most of the day.

GAIL *laughs*.

GAIL   I took it off when they buried us.

KAREN   That's right. I forgot that.

GAIL   The sand got everywhere.

KAREN   Two heads popping above a blanket of sand.

GAIL   There was a photo of that, I think.

KAREN   You moaned the whole day.
            The sand hurt your feet.
            Got in the fur of your coat.

GAIL   We had egg sandwiches.
            I remember that.
            Egg sandwiches…

KAREN   …that crunched with sand…

GAIL   …and warm squash.
            Rocko Roberts told us to bury the bottle,
            remember.

KAREN   Bury the bottle to keep the squash cold.

GAIL   It was warm.

KAREN   It was warm.

GAIL   And covered in grit and sand.

KAREN   And that game? What was it?

GAIL   Rounders.
            I hated that game.

KAREN   You and your coat stood as far away from the game
            as you could.

GAIL   I was fielding.

KAREN   Is that what you call it?

GAIL   I was thinking ahead in case of a huge strike and
            then I'd be in place to stop a sixer.

KAREN   You were sat far enough away so that no one could
            see you smoking, is what you were doing.

            KAREN *laughs*.

GAIL   He's dead.

KAREN   Who?

GAIL   Rocko.

            I went to his funeral.

            He died last year.

KAREN   I didn't know that.

GAIL   His wife was there. And his son. His daughters.
            Grandchildren. They were devastated. Hundreds of
            people were there.
            I had a thought that I might go to the front of the
            church and punch his photo off his coffin. Tell
            everyone what a wanker he was.
            But.
            I was late. I went in.
            Sat at the back.

            His coffin was small. I remembered him being
            so big.

I thought. He must have been ill. For it to be so small. He must have been ill.

I hope he suffered.

I thought about you.

KAREN   You shouldn't have.

GAIL   I did.

I thought about you a lot, as it happens.
Over the years.

I never stopped thinking about you.

KAREN   Jesus, Gail.

GAIL   You was always in here. (*Head.*)

They look at each other.

I found you now though.

Pause.

They hold a look.

I thought, Kaz.
I thought,
you know,
us,
I thought we could.
I thought we could start over or something.

Lets that settle.

KAREN *doesn't respond for a while.*

In that silence GAIL notes the rejection of that idea.

KAREN   I think you should leave now, Gail.

It's been nice catching up but I need to go.

GAIL *processes everything.*

GAIL   Karen.

KAREN   I'm going to phone down to let Bill know we're
         finished here and the office is clear.

GAIL   Karen. There was something, Kaz.

         KAREN picks up a phone and buzzes to reception.

         See, I wouldn't ask unless I was… I need your
         help, Kaz.

KAREN   (*To phone.*) Hi Bill,

GAIL   Karen?

KAREN   (*To phone.*) Yep. On my way.

         KAREN watches GAIL.

         Actually, Bill, there's someone here with me so
         there'll be
         two of us leaving.
         That's right.

         No. Everyone else has gone.

GAIL   I just. There's something I need to ask.

KAREN   (*To phone.*) Thanks, Bill.

         Puts down phone, waits for GAIL to speak.

GAIL   So.
         Yes.
         Yeah, well
         It's awkward a bit

         I just

KAREN   What?

GAIL   I dunno now, feels a bit…

         See the thing is.

         Pause.

         I wanted to see you. I did. I told you I looked for you.
         I didn't give up. I just.
         Life throws things at you.

I had kids of my own.
And time flies, don't it.
Years go by.
I really wanted to see you.

KAREN   Well, you've seen me, Gail.

GAIL   Yeah.

KAREN   Okay.

GAIL   Yeah, okay.

The thing is…

Takes a breath.

KAREN   Just say it.
Whatever it is just say it.

GAIL   D'you love your kids?

Stops.

Course you do.

I love my kids. Just like you.

Look, you haven't got time for this, I know.
You need to get home.
So I'll keep it short.

I got myself into some bother. Always been in
bother, you know me. And I got mixed up in things.
I never had money. I nicked a bit. Stupid stuff and
I got caught. And ended up inside. But there's no
one else. Just me. I had no one could look after my
boys so.
They put them with this family.
While I was away.
And now.
I'm getting on-track.

But there's a care order. You knows all about that
stuff.
I got to turn things round, you know, if I wants that
to change.

If I wants my kids back.
And I want my kids back.
I can't leave 'em there.
Not like they did to us. Cos we know, don't we.
What happens.

And see,
The job I had, it was a shit job, I've had loads of
jobs, all shit, nothing fancy like you but this time,
it was everything. I can't tell you.

I had to get up.
At the right time.
I had to get dressed and get there.

And I had a laugh with the girls there. So it was
good. It was good for me. I was getting on alright.
I was.
Don't seem like much
It was, though.

Kept me in a routine.

Stopped my mind from wandering.

So I lost it anyway. I lost my job.

It's like.
It never rains, does it?
But. For my kids.

I'm here for my kids. You know.

KAREN   You're here for your kids?

GAIL   I am, yeah.

KAREN   That's why you're here?

GAIL   It is.

I thought with what you do, I thought you could
help me.

With my situation.

You could do something.

KAREN takes it in.

Half-laughs.

KAREN   Oh, you think…

GAIL   I'm asking you to help me.
I need my kids, Kaz.
I'm not coping without them.

KAREN realises GAIL means it.

KAREN   You think because I work here?

GAIL   You're Head of Children's Services.

KAREN   What and so you think I can wave my magic wand
and get your kids back for you?

GAIL   I thought you could have a look at my case.

KAREN   Oh yeah, hang on, I'll just make a phone call,
round them up for you.
For Christ's sake.

I can't even begin to explain the many, many issues
I have with what you've just asked of me. Just you
being here is…

GAIL   I thought you might be able to –

KAREN   What?

What did you think?

GAIL   I dunno. Something. I thought you could do
something. It's my kids. I thought.

KAREN   I protect children, Gail. I protect them.
You being here is a conflict of interest, do you
understand that.
Do you even know what that is?
So while you're stood there telling me, making
demands of me, I'm trying to work out where all
this stands procedurally…

I. We…
Okay, listen.

Takes a breath.

We don't take children away from their mothers on
a whim.
That's just not possible.
It doesn't happen.
There are reasons you are not with your children.
Valid and serious reasons.

And you don't get your kids back as a favour
because you know someone who can pull a few
strings.
That's not how this works.

Pause.

GAIL   When I was sat out there waiting.
I read this magazine.
And they was saying there was this thing.
About the brain. About addiction. And it's
fascinating.
It says they thinks there's a bit of the brain.
A special place in the brain where people feels
pleasure.
It's the part that if you was an alcoholic, when you
drink, this is the bit that makes you feel like a
million dollars.
This bit is the bit that tells you that you need have
another one cos it wants to feel that feeling again,
you know.
Same for drugs. Chocolate. Sex.
All of them good things.
And in tests, this is what they said anyway, in tests
when the brain is doing the good stuff, this bit of
the brain reacts, it hits the pleasure dome and then
some.
And you know what they found.
They found the same part of the brain reacted in the
same way when mothers look at photographs of
their kids.
We get that, don't we.

Us mothers. Most of us, anyhow.
But what that makes you realise if you think about
it, is that it's not just that we love our kids.
It's that we're addicted to them.
Our brain tells us we can't live without them.
We don't just want them.
We need them.
It's a different thing.
I need my kids.
Need them.

KAREN   Gail.
Look.
What I suggest is.
I suggest you.
I suggest you…
You need to sort yourself out. You need to get a job.

GAIL   I had a job.

KAREN   Get another one.

GAIL   Look at me.

KAREN   You could get a job.

GAIL   You wanna give me one?

KAREN   Seriously.

GAIL   I could be your PA.
Do a better job than that one you got.

KAREN   I doubt that.

GAIL   Or cleaning then?

KAREN   Stop it.

GAIL   What? I'm not too proud to clean, Kaz. I've got
that, you know, the OCD so I'm very particular
with things. I shower sometimes three times a day.
I'm good at floors.

KAREN   What?

GAIL   That's my thing. Floors. The floors would be
              spotless.

              I could do your house? I'm not far from where
              you live.

KAREN   You don't know where I live.

GAIL   I can do odd jobs an' all?
              Put my hand to anything. Them old houses need
              looking after.

KAREN   I have a man who sees to that stuff.

GAIL   I could help you out a bit with your kids? It's a fair
              walk to that school of theirs. And it's hard to get
              people you can trust?

KAREN   I don't need your help, Gail.

GAIL   I need yours.

              They hold a look.

              Hold.

              KAREN *drops her eyes.*

              Thinks.

              Realises.

KAREN   You know where I live.

GAIL   Must take you some time to get over here, from
              where you are?

KAREN   Have you been to my house?

GAIL   That why you work so late, is it? So you miss the
              traffic?

KAREN   You've been to my house?

GAIL   He works late, your husband.

              Does he always get home after dark?

KAREN   What?

GAIL   Do he get home that time every night?

KAREN   You've been to my home.

GAIL   I was going to say hello to him but I didn't know if
          he knows about me.

          KAREN *takes that in.*

KAREN   Well, he knows about you so if you think that's in
          some way a threat, Gail...

GAIL   What does he know?

KAREN   When did you go to my house?

GAIL   I been there a few times.

KAREN   I don't want you there.

GAIL   He knows about me.

KAREN   Yes.

GAIL   You said he didn't know.

KAREN   Well, he does. So.

GAIL   What did you tell him?

KAREN   I told him I had a sister.

GAIL   You have a sister.

          Pause.

          What else?

KAREN   I told him we don't know each other, okay? That
          we hadn't seen each other since we were kids.

GAIL   What did he say?

KAREN   Nothing.

GAIL   Nothing?

KAREN   He said nothing.

GAIL   Did you tell him about our life?

KAREN   Why would I?

GAIL   Did you tell him we were close?

KAREN   We weren't close.

GAIL   We were.

Pause.

GAIL   When did you tell him?

KAREN   When?

GAIL   When you first met him?

KAREN   No.

GAIL   Yesterday?

KAREN   Of course not.

GAIL   When?

KAREN   I don't remember.

GAIL   You do.

KAREN   He knows about you. He's known for years.

Pause.

GAIL   When I was pregnant the first thing I thought of was you. Always in my mind you was.

I think you told him when you was pregnant.

Pause.

Course you did.

KAREN   I don't want you near my house.

GAIL   Why not?

KAREN   Because it's fucking weird. Stalky. And we both know you've got previous in that department or have you forgotten about Suzanne Cox?

GAIL   You told him about me when you were pregnant because as hard as you tried you couldn't forget it or me.

How old is she?

KAREN   Who?

GAIL   Your oldest.

KAREN   What?

GAIL   Ten? / Eleven?

KAREN   She's ten.

GAIL   Did you tell him what happened to you?

           Pause.

           Did you tell him?

KAREN   I told him it was the worst
           The absolute worst time of my life.
           How I hated it.
           It was a nightmare.
           A living nightmare
           Getting through the day. Surviving.
           It was survival.
           I told him about the relief when I got away
           The place.
           The stink of it.
           How when I got to Wales I felt like I breathed for
           the first time.
           Fresh air
           I could finally breathe.
           Sleep at night

           That's what I told him.

GAIL   What did he say?

KAREN   He said he
           He said that it all made sense.

           Why I live for my work.
           He understood it then.
           I work
           My work is important to me
           Because I know what it's like to be in care.
           To live that life.
           He said, I know how it feels.

GAIL *laughs*.

It's not funny, Gail.

GAIL   No. You're right. But it is though.

KAREN   None of this is funny.

GAIL   It is to me though.

KAREN   Stop grinning.

GAIL   Sorry, Kaz. You an' him making sense of it all.

GAIL *scoffs*.

I think it's fucking hilarious.

KAREN   I think you're a fucking idiot.

KAREN goes through her bag.

Gets out her purse.

Has a wad of notes in her hand.

Okay, so look
Well this has been interesting it really has and I'm
sorry for you
How it turned out
This
That your life has gone to shit
But
And I am sorry, Gail, truly
But I'm not your...
You're not my responsibility.

She puts the notes into a bewildered GAIL's hands.

I want you to have this.
Call it a gesture.
But then I want you to go.

Cos let's be honest here
We don't know each other at all, do we.
Come on, Gail, really?
We're strangers actually.
And that's okay. It is what it is.

GAIL *looks at the notes*.

You shouldn't have come here Gail, you /
shouldn't.

GAIL   Look.
I shouldn't have come to your work, I'm sorry
about that.
I know I shouldn't have come here.

KAREN   No. It's not that.

Takes a deep breath.

I'm going to be very clear with you now okay
because I think it's important. I want you to
understand where I'm at.

I don't want to see you again.

I have a family. My family. A beautiful home.
Holidays. My life is happy. Joyful.

That person you talk about. Karen. That's not me.
Kaz?
I don't remember her. She never really existed.
You've made some picture in your head about us.
Sisters. But she's a figment of your imagination.

I don't want you in my life.

I really don't.

Do you understand?

Pause.

Lets that settle.

Gail. Do you understand me?

GAIL   Yes.

KAREN   Good.

GAIL   I understand you.

KAREN   It's for the best I think. Because you and me. It's
not good.

KAREN's phone buzzes.

That'll be Bill.

I'm sorry, Gail.

GAIL *looks at the money in her hand.*

KAREN *picks up her bag.*

Moves to leave.

Please.

Shows GAIL *the door.*

After you.

GAIL *looks back to the money. Places it on the desk.*

Looks around her.

Takes a moment.

Takes a seat.

GAIL   You know I feel a bit…

KAREN   What?

GAIL   It's my head.
My ears.
I get a bit spinny.

KAREN   Do you.
Right.
Well, perhaps you should get some fresh air.

GAIL   I just need to sit here. Just gimme five minutes.

KAREN *checks her watch.*

Knows she's being played but…

Sighs.

KAREN   Five minutes.

GAIL *holds her head in her hands.*

Breathes deep.

Sits back in the chair.

Takes in her surroundings.

GAIL   You know. It's a lovely old building is this.

KAREN *watches her.*

You find them don't you. In the old docks.
These great old buildings.
Remember that one down the old docks, Kaz, we
used to play in.

Dorian there used to say he'd seen the ghost.
The white lady. Remember?
There's always a ghost, isn't there.
He said she walked at night with a crying baby in
a shawl.

Laughs to herself.

Always a white lady, the ghosts, aren't they?
Always a baby somewhere.

Pause.

What did this used to be, Kaz? Before it was
council?

Nothing.

There's a whatsit on the front, as you go in,
established 1842 or whatever.
Same as on that school your kids goes to. Above
the main door in the stone.

I wonder what it started out as?
Yeah.
I wonder.

KAREN *takes a deep breath. Puts down her bag.*

There'll be a record somewhere of how it started,
what happened to it. There always is with things.

KAREN   You've been to their school.

GAIL   Bet it costs a fortune to upkeep though.
              Probably riddled with damp an' all sorts.

KAREN   You were at my children's school?

              GAIL *looks at* KAREN.

GAIL   Is it one of them private schools where they go?
              Looked like.
              Bet it costs a fortune to send your kids there.

KAREN   I don't want you near my kids.

GAIL   It's all about money. Everything's different if you
              got it, you know. There's different rules.

KAREN   It's a school, for Christ's sake. They're my
              children.

GAIL   They say it don't make you happy but that's a
              fucking lie. Like when they says to kids nits only
              lives in clean hair, remember they used to say that
              to us and we was stinking most of the time. It's the
              same. Fucking lies.
              If you got money it's just easier.

KAREN   I can give you money.

              Pause.

GAIL   There'll be all sorts of important kids goes to that
              school, I bet.
              Russians and all that. Famous people. Or Royals
              even. I bet Royals goes there, do they? Diana's
              kids, what they called.
              I don't want your money.

KAREN   You need help.
              I can't help you.

GAIL   Wills innit. William and Kate. Their kids. Do they
              go there, I wonder?

KAREN   You can't come into my life. I didn't ask you. You
              can't barge into my life.

GAIL   He's lovely him. That Sweet William.

KAREN   Please don't underestimate me, Gail.

GAIL   The other one though. With the ginger hair. He's
              not a nice fella I don't think.
              He's not nice in all the right ways, I don't think.

              GAIL *laughs*.

KAREN   I know what you're capable of.

GAIL   Wouldn't kick him outta bed, would you, Kaz?

KAREN   You know what I'm capable of.

GAIL   He's filthy they reckon.
              The ginger one.

              GAIL *chuckles to herself*.

KAREN   I'm giving you a chance to walk away. Before this
              escalates.

              Stops.

GAIL   They lost their mother though, didn't they?
              Don't matter who you are.
              They'll have felt it the same. The pain of
              separation.
              Mother and child.

              Escalates?

KAREN   Suzanne Cox moved away in the end. Her whole
              family upped and left.
              Because of you.

GAIL   I did wonder where she got to.

KAREN   You hounded her.

GAIL   I didn't hound no one.

KAREN   All over that stupid game.
              At her house, all hours of the day and night. You cut
              off her hair. I remember that.

Her poor parents.
And still you went there. Couldn't give a shit.

GAIL   Her mother hit me. Slapped me across the head.
            And no offence but she was built like a brick
            shithouse.

KAREN   But it was me that got it in the neck.
            Always me, wasn't it.
            I had to promise Roberts to keep you out of their
            way. And you know what happened to me if I didn't
            do what they wanted. I wasted my childhood keeping
            you out of people's way. Taking the rap for you.

GAIL   We looked out for each other.

KAREN   I mopped up after you.

GAIL   I just wanted to be her friend.

KAREN   That's not how you make friends.

GAIL   She had stuff. All the stuff she had, Kaz, you
            remember?

KAREN   You stole from her. All her things. Anything you
            wanted you took. The Nintendo was the last straw.

GAIL   I borrowed her stuff.

KAREN   You never gave it back.

GAIL   She let me have it.

KAREN   She was terrified of you.

GAIL   She was my friend.

KAREN   You took whatever you wanted and when she told
            on you, you cut off her hair.

GAIL   It wasn't like that.

            Pause.

            That babysitter that picks up your kids?

KAREN   What about her?

GAIL   What is she? Polish or something?

KAREN   She's their nanny.

GAIL   I didn't know who she was.

KAREN   Why would you, for Christ's sake?

GAIL   She couldn't speak English whoever she was.

KAREN   Jesus. Look at you. Sat there with no shame in you.

GAIL   Shame?

KAREN   You were hanging around a school.

GAIL   I wasn't hanging around.

KAREN   You know, I worked in a school. They would have
         known you were there. They would have seen you.

GAIL   I wanted to see them.

KAREN   I would have called the police. The state of you.
         I'm surprised they didn't call the police.
         Did you even think about that? The impact that
         would have on your situation.

         Course you didn't.

GAIL   I told the babysitter who I was.

KAREN   You approached her?

GAIL   I said I was your sister.

KAREN   They were there? Were they there?

GAIL   She was waiting for them. I saw her with them the
         day before.

KAREN   You could have been anyone.
         You would have confused her.

GAIL   She looked confused way before I got to her.

KAREN   You're a stranger.

GAIL   I told her, straight away.

KAREN   Some strange woman approaches her…

GAIL   I told her I'm your sister. Strange?

KAREN   You're not my sister.
            I have a sister-in-law. She thinks that's my sister.

GAIL   She don't speak no English anyway so confusing
            her…

KAREN   You wanted to see them so you went there. Then
            you go back.

GAIL   She weren't all there in the head if you ask me.

KAREN   Why would you go back?

GAIL   I wouldn't feel right if she was looking after my
            kids is all I'm saying.

            KAREN *scoffs*.

KAREN   I've heard it all now. Your kids are in care. You
            don't know who is looking after them.

GAIL   I was looking out for them.

KAREN   What?

GAIL   The kids.

KAREN   Oh yeah. That's right. People like you are always
            looking out for your kids.

GAIL   People like me.

KAREN   Save it, Gail, cos I've heard a million 'I love my
            kids' stories.
            I know you.
            You lost your boys because you were neglectful.

GAIL   Not mine.

KAREN   You fucked up. Surprise, surprise. Couldn't even
            look after your own kids.
            Simple.

GAIL   You're not listening. Not my kids.

            Pause.

KAREN   Who were you looking out for?

GAIL   The girl.

KAREN   What girl?

GAIL   Your babysitter.

KAREN   What about her?

GAIL   Nah. It's nothing.

KAREN		GAIL	
Stop it.		GAIL	No, it's not
I don't want to			I won't
hear			You're right
I'm not playing			It's not my
Stupid games			business.

    Stop fucking around.

GAIL   She was sharp with the little one.
That's why I went back.
I was there.
I know you think I shouldn't but
You wasn't there.
I was.

She shouts at the little one cos she's not moving
fast enough or whatever
Frightening her
She grabbed her
Pulled her by her arm
Which was harsh I thought
And your little one, she starts to cry.

KAREN *says nothing*.

Takes it in.

GAIL   I felt sorry for them.

KAREN   Don't.

GAIL   They looked sad.

KAREN   What a load of bullshit.

GAIL   It's true though.

KAREN   Absolute bullshit.

GAIL   She was sharp with her.

KAREN   You're full of it.
              Full of shit.

GAIL   They're not happy.

KAREN   What are you talking about?

GAIL   Your kids aren't happy is what I'm talking about.

KAREN   Are you actually going to stand there and lecture
              me about child welfare?

GAIL   They got briefcases of homework bigger than what
              they are.
              How old is the little one? Four? Five?
              Picked up by some nanny or au pair what they
              hardly know.

KAREN   My children are extremely happy. They have
              a perfect childhood.

GAIL   I never left my kids with no one. They went
              everywhere with me.

              Even the pub.

              Laughs.

              Your face.

              Seriously though. When did that come to be
              a crime?

              How old is the little one, four?

KAREN   It's good for them to experience independence.

GAIL   Yeah. There we are then.

KAREN   My daughters have a hard-working woman with
              a fulfilling career as their role model.

GAIL   But all a kid really wants is its mum though. That's
        the thing.

        Pause.

KAREN   Or its dad. Not that you'd ever consider that.
        D'you even know who your boys' fathers are?

GAIL   I'll bet your little one sees you for what? For half
        an hour a day.
        If they're lucky that is.

KAREN   Blindly assailing the choices of childcare at the
        woman.
        So predictable.
        Course it's normal for a father to put his career
        first, nobody blinks.
        Absolutely monstrous for a mother, I get it.

GAIL   Your babysitter's bringing up your kids, Kaz.

KAREN   She's their nanny. For fuck's sake.

        Takes a minute, thinks, then begins to laugh.

        *As she talks she starts looking through a filing
        cabinet/drawers.*

        Look at you. Stood there like you have the moral
        high ground. You're hilarious.

        KAREN *is frenetically looking for something.*

        You know, Gail.

        I forgot how funny you were.

        Papers drop and files are thrown.

GAIL   It's okay though. They'll grow up to be all
        successful. Because Mummy have paid for that to
        be the way.

        If bankers and lawyers and politicians is what you
        rates as successful that is, cos in my opinion, Kaz,
        they're generally a bunch of wankers.

But mostly the kids end up all messed up inside cos
the truth of it is their mummy didn't give a shit
after all.

You know what I think.
If I'm honest with you, Karen.

I think it's neglectful.

KAREN *stops looking and starts listening.*

KAREN   Really.

GAIL   However you dress it up.
Okay, it's different to my neglect.
Cos all the people making the rules and laws never
lived my life. They got no idea how much it takes
for me to get through the day.
Like I said, it's all about money, money makes
the rules.
And of course it's judgement. She judges she,
judges she, judges her. Sad that. We do it to
ourselves, women.
To make ourselves feel better, I reckon.

What am I saying? That's your job innit,
judgement.

That's what I thinks anyway.

KAREN   But you see, I really don't care what you think.

Takes a bit of time with that.

I didn't work when they were little.
Those first years.
I was so desperate, so utterly desperate for
settlement and security. It was pathetic.
When I look back on it now, I was pathetic.
I joined all the clubs. NCT and tumble tots and
soft-play and daisy wrigglers and yes – Yumi Yoga.
It was mind-numbing. All the smiling. At other
people's kids. At each other.

Days filled with trivialities.

Endless hours, talking about what time the children get up in the morning, how often the bedlinen is changed, weaning, milestones, eco-friendly cleaning products and wooden toys. And let me tell you, breast-feeding was NOT one of the most rewarding or incredible experiences of *my* life. Every day the expectation to perform an impossible job.

The idealisation of motherhood, the perfect mother, wife, who is good, who is virtuous, who must create a chocolate-box world in which to place her refined-sugar-free children, whilst smiling benignly from behind her vintage teak dresser and her freshly pressed Whistles blouse. But hey, don't worry, she's still cool enough to know her Kanye from her Jay-Z and easily knocks up an impromptu risotto or frittata for 'friends'. She even ironically drinks Aldi prosecco before fulfilling blowjob duty to her eternally eligible husband at least once a week.

Utter bollocks.

I hadn't felt so needy. So dependent. Since…

I can't be dependent. I won't. I can provide for myself and my children.

I was a fraud. I was being asked to do things I hated. Daily. By the hour.
Being told who I was, who I was allowed to be.

I neglected me. That's who I neglected, Gail.
When I went back to work, I felt joy.
I was supposed to feel shame but I felt free.

We're all just trying to do our best.
I do my best.

GAIL   I try to do my best.
            But sometimes there's too much shit being thrown your way. You can't dodge it in the end.

KAREN   We all have our shit.

GAIL   But people like me, Kaz, we don't have the luxury of foreign babysitters and posh expensive schools to dig us out of the shit when we have kids we can't look after.

KAREN   I can look after them.

GAIL   You don't.

KAREN   I choose not to. And I'm alright with that.

GAIL   Nice to have choices.

KAREN   I've had times when I didn't.

GAIL   They don't know you.

KAREN   Know me?

GAIL   They lost you.

KAREN   They don't lose me. They gain me. You wouldn't understand that.

GAIL   You neglect them. That's what I think.

KAREN   Now who's judging?

    And for the record, my job isn't about judgement. It's about care. Support. I help people.

GAIL   Then help me.

    Pause.

KAREN   When I first got pregnant I was terrified. You can imagine. Everyone is, aren't they. But for kids like us…

    I didn't think I could love it enough.

    Pause.

    I married young.
    Straight out of college.

I was a teacher. When I was first married.
I hated it.

You know what I hated the most?

GAIL *says nothing*.

Accessories.

Hats, gloves, scarves, bags.
They were the bain of my life.
Thirty-two five-year-olds, all looking for a lost
glove or bag. Bobbles, clips, hairbands. Jesus
Christ.
The tediousness of it all.

One day, I was sat watching the class, they were
getting on with a task or whatever and there were
two girls, Laura and Beth. Best friends. They
started messing about with each other's hair,
playing, you know. Like girls do. Laura undid
Beth's hairband and ran her fingers through Beth's
hair. Properly running her fingers through using her
whole hand like it was a comb.
And Beth's hair is long, halfway down her back.
And Laura's got her fingers right in and she's
wrapping the hair around and around her hand and
then in a flash and without any warning, she grabs
hold of all the hair in her hand and pulls it, really
nastily.
With a smile too.
So I got up and I went over to them and I grabbed
a handful of Laura's hair, and I pull her hair back,
really hard.
I felt her head yank with the force. And her little
fingers grabbed for my hand but I kept on pulling.
It was only when I saw that her feet were off the
ground that I stopped.
I didn't want to stop.
But eventually I let go and Laura drops to the floor.
And I had a handful of her hair in my hand.

She cried.
Screamed.
The whole class was silent and staring at me.
And Beth throws her arms around Laura and kisses
her, hugs her, tells her everything would be okay
and then shoots me a look like I was the devil.
The whole class looked at me like I was the devil.
Which I was, of course. I didn't feel sorry straight
away. For a moment I felt like I'd done them a
favour. Like I'd shown them that life is cruel. And
unexpected. And startling.

The anger still startles me.
It doesn't go.
It might sit dormant for a while but there are
unexplained, unexpected times when it rears itself.
I hate that.

Takes her time.

I walked out.
Out of the classroom and through the hall and
across the yard, through the gates.

I went home.

Then I felt sorry.

I was going to leave.
Everything.
I was going to give up.
My husband.

But I was pregnant. This baby. Made from love.
Inside me.

And I couldn't.
For the first time in my life I couldn't run.

I had something much more important than myself
to think about. I realised that I already loved it
enough.
I thought that whatever happened, I would never
run again.

I would stay.
For the baby. For the child.
I wanted my baby to have a childhood, so badly.
And even if I could give it nothing else then I
would give it that. My child would wake up with
its mother and father, every day. It would sleep
soundly in a bed knowing that it was safe.
Protected by the only two people in the world who
would die for it, without question.

We owe our children that, Gail.
It's the least. The very least of it.
I gave my girls that. I give my girls that.
Unconditionally.

You have to help yourself. It's the only way.

I won't help you any more.

GAIL   Any more?

              Pause.

KAREN   Next time you're at my girl's school or anywhere
              near my home.
              I'll fucking kill you.

              They hold a look.

              We know KAREN *means this.*

GAIL   Did you look for him?

KAREN   Who?

GAIL   Your son?

              Did you ever even look for him?

              Pause.

              KAREN *takes that in, rooted to the spot.*

              I didn't think so.
              I know *he* weren't made from *love.* But we can't
              all be.

KAREN   Get out.

GAIL   I think about him all the time.

KAREN   I want you out of here.

GAIL   Working here.
          You would know where he was.
          Wouldn't be able to stop yourself from finding out
          about him.

          Where is he?
          Who is he with?
          Is he okay?
          Happy?
          Did it work out okay for him?
          It does don't it, sometimes.

KAREN   I'll call the police.

GAIL   You says it was always you that was looking after
          me, Kaz, mopping after me but that's not how
          I remembers it.
          That's not how I remembers it at all.

KAREN   Fuck off. D'you hear me? Go on, fuck off.

GAIL   I covered for you all the time. Unconditionally.

KAREN   You never covered for me.

GAIL   Because you was my sister.

KAREN   I took it all for you. What they did to me.

GAIL   I helped you.

KAREN   I took the beatings for both of us.

          It was me he…
          Me.

          It was me.
          Not you.

          And you stand there.

GAIL   It was you who I woke up to every day.

KAREN   I took it so you didn't have to.

           Stop.

GAIL   A baby. It wasn't his fault.
           I was there for you.
           With you.
           I was there by your side for all of it.
           I'd do anything for you.

KAREN   I was thirteen, for Christ's sake.

GAIL   I was there when they took him off you. A beautiful
           little boy. We held him.
           You and me.
           It was beautiful.
           Remember, Kaz?

KAREN   I remember mess. And bodies. And people looking
           at me. I was a child. I remember mucus and blood
           and dirt and shit and vomit and noise and smells
           and pain.
           I don't remember beauty.

GAIL   My heart broke, same as yours.

KAREN   I didn't want him.
           Don't presume my heart was broken.
           He grew inside me, that's all.
           Things grow inside us that we don't want. That
           happens.
           Because of this – (*Boobs*.)
           This – (*Vag*.)
           I'm supposed to love something like that.
           To love him?
           How could I love him?
           How?
           I prayed that he would die. Begged God. Any god.
           Night after night, I wanted him dead.
           I was drinking, I took pills and he still lived.
           Grew.

He kept growing.
Like a cancer.

Pause.

The day he was born I realised something.
I realised that I wasn't just creating a life.
I was also creating a death.
Because with a life comes a death. One day he
would die. And that made it okay.
When they took him.
I was glad.

The intercom buzzes.

KAREN *grabs for the phone.*

Kate Taylor.

GAIL   You talk about a child's rights.

KAREN   Hi, Bill.

GAIL   What about his rights, Kaz?

KAREN   Bill, yes I'm here.

GAIL   To know his mother? That's what you said. A child's
            rights to know its parents.

KAREN   No.
            Don't come up.
            It's fine.
            We're fine.

GAIL   What about his childhood?

KAREN   I got held up. I'm fine. Yes.

GAIL   He's part of us. Do you care about that?

            Looks to GAIL.

KAREN   She's with me. We're leaving. Now.

            KAREN *puts down the phone.*

            KAREN *starts gathering her things frenetically.*

In amongst gathering her things she picks up a file.

Finally found it.

KAREN *opens the file and reads from it.*

On August the 4th and 12th the mother, Gail
Palmer, had prearranged meetings that she failed to
attend. Both children were obviously upset…

GAIL *grabs for the folder. Papers start to fall.*

Both KAREN *and* GAIL *grab for the papers.*

They scuffle a bit. Starting with GAIL *trying to stop*
KAREN *from leaving.*

Ending with KAREN *getting rough with* GAIL.

*A shove too hard leads into a slap, a punch, a fight,
two kids, sisters scraping lead by* KAREN.

KAREN *lays into a submissive* GAIL, *ending with*
KAREN *holding* GAIL *by the hair.*

KAREN *stops.*

Nina Simone starts quietly.

GAIL *moves into* KAREN, *holds on to her.*

Holds her.

Breathes her in.

KAREN *doesn't hold her but maybe relaxes into*
GAIL, *maybe puts her head on her shoulder. They
slowly move together, rotate slowly, as if in a slow
dance. Some elements from their childish dance
might be echoed here.*
Give this time for us to feel it, to see them.

KAREN *lifts her head, gently pulls away.*

*Takes a moment and pulls herself together. Brushes
down her clothes.*

*Picks up a sheet of paper from the floor and starts
reading.*

On August the 4th and 12th the mother, Gail Palmer, had prearranged meetings that she failed to attend. Both children were obviously upset and it was decided that one further meeting would be arranged before action to cease visitation would be taken. Unfortunately, due to unforeseen circumstances, once again the mother, Gail Palmer, failed to attend. It was decided under some duress to refer the case back to Children's services for consideration. Although the general consensus was thought to be visitation rights for the mother should cease in order to protect the children from further harm, the head of Children's Services, Kate Taylor, overruled the decision and made a stipulation for supervised visits to be strongly encouraged and supported as the mother, Gail Palmer, had shown commendable attempts to rebuild her life. Securing accommodation and gaining permanent employment.

KAREN *lets the paper fall to the floor.*

Starts to leave.

GAIL *grabs for her.*

KAREN *stops.*

GAIL *slowly lets her go.*

KAREN *leaves.*

Doesn't look back.

GAIL *is alone.*

Nina Simone plays.

Taking us into…

Three

The Factory

There is less confusion and chaos in this scene, although it should still be there just less.

A radio can play. On and off. Nina Simone songs still come in and out. Again a variety but without 'My Baby Just Cares for Me' within the mix. White noise and levels of louder volume as and when useful to suggest absurdity. A buzz might be helpful. The lights might flicker/dim.

Between her dialogue, which is directed at random members of the audience, GAIL *will do all or some of the following:*

Wait.

Fidget.

Sit up and down, out and in, of the chair.

Pick at herself.

Drum her fingers.

Jump.

Turn around.

Turn and stand with her back to the audience.

Sniff.

Fuss her hair.

Circle the space.

Sniff again.

Clear her throat.

Be bothered by her nose.

Whistle.

Wipe her nose with the back of her hand.

Look at the back of her hand. Shit, shouldn't have done that.

Wipe her hand in her skirt.

Look around.

Rub down her clothes.

GAIL *is onstage. Alone. Waiting. She paces. Circles. In her own time she finds her place. Directs her dialogue at audience members. Using all of the audience. Moving at the reset.*

GAIL   I wasn't sure where to wait so.

           I called.

           Pardon?

           When I got the letter.

           Yeah?

           You said I could appeal my dismissal.

           Sounds break in.

           GAIL *resets.*

           Oh.

           I didn't realise.

           It's all there.

           In the letter. I wrote it all down.

           Like you said.

           You said I could appeal.

           And that's what I did.

           Sounds break in.

           GAIL *resets.*

           I was going to leave it.

           But then I thought…

           I wrote it all down.

It's all there.

You said I had thirty days.

It's all in the letter there.

I wrote that.

Sounds break in.

GAIL *resets.*

Will you give that to him?

Mr Silver? The boss?

He's alright, I heard. Kind.

Will you give him the letter?

I need a job.

You'll tell him, I liked it here. I did.

I swear, I won't let you down, if you just give me
a chance.

Sounds break in.

GAIL *resets.*

Does it work? When you appeal?

Nobody?

I don't give up easy.

I'm like a dog with a bone, me, that's what they say.

No. I don't say that in the letter.

I say that I'm sorry. That's what I say. It says in
there how sorry I am.

And that I'm going to try.

I'm going to try hard.

Yeah, well I'm sure you have heard it all before but
this time it's different.

Why?

Pause.

Looks down thinks a bit.

Looks up, directly at an audience member.

This time I mean it.

Silence.

GAIL *is alone.*

Sniffs.

Fusses her hair.

Sniffs again.

Clears her throat.

GAIL *stands.*

Straight.

Smiles to herself.

Holds her head high.

Confident.

Head held high.

Sniffs.

Looks around.

Blackout.

The End.

A Nick Hern Book

Thick As Thieves first published in Great Britain in 2018 as a paperback original by Nick Hern Books Limited, The Glasshouse, 49a Goldhawk Road, London W12 8QP, in association with Clean Break and Theatr Clwyd

Cover image by Sarah Ferrari, www.sarahferrari.com

Designed and typeset by Nick Hern Books, London
Printed in the UK by Mimeo Ltd, Huntingdon, Cambridgeshire PE29 6XX

A CIP catalogue record for this book is available from the British Library

ISBN 978 1 84842 776 1